My Voice: Faced wit' ^ ..

Written by:

Daniel Williams

My Voice: Faced with Autism

By Daniel Williams

Dedication

I want to first dedicate this book to my parents, Jacqueline and Robert, who have always believed in me. I would not be where I am today without my parents. I know they are not here on Earth anymore but they are watching over me and still present. I have them in my heart and mind forever. I thank you guys for believing in me when no one else did.

CONTENTS

Chapter 7

My experience living with Autism

Chapter 8

My growth as Daniel

Chapter 9

My voice for the Future

Introduction

My Life starts here and Now

This goes all the way back when I was in high school, when I became an adult. When I was eighteen, I really went through a lot as my world was getting easier, but it was also getting harder. I was dealing with a lot of emotions because I have a disability that I never realized I had. It was my life that helped me go on and it was what made me realize that I was a normal human being. I never faulted for the things I could have done for myself. I had no worries about a job, a car or my own place (like most teens at eighteen were doing.)

I want to give my readers a glimpse of what I have gone through and want to share my story about my life challenges. This is me being me and writing about my experience. This is my true self and I am pouring my life in this book. I want anyone who reads this to know me for who I am. This has taken me time to think and process about what I want to write in this book. It has taken me since January 2016 to compress my thoughts. I am writing this book as a way for me to help not only myself but for other people as well. I can go on and on about this section of the book but it is the beginning of the book.

Chapter 1
My Parents

My parents got married in 2006 and had known each other for some time. To make a long story short, it felt like they were together forever. My mom was a no-nonsense type of woman. If you got to know her, then you would see her as a loving and caring woman. She lived as if you'd disrespect her, she would have gone off. She'd let you know how it is and wouldn't bite her tongue. I loved my mom. She fought hard for her family and made sure no one bothered me.

This was when I was living on Winter Street. Those were my roots and I embraced my culture. I grew up where there were many stores and a lot of those stores were owned by Middle Eastern and African American men. Some of the stores included 99 cent shops, barbershops, and liquor stores. I would go to the Pontiac Mall in the neighborhood. It was far from my house but convenient. I like that place because there were always people to hang out with. One time after I was picked on by this boy, he punched me in the mouth. I wanted to fight back but I was not going to let my bike go. There really was nothing I could do after I got hit because the guy was gone. I told my mom about it and no lie; she ran out of the house with no shoes and went back to where the dude was. She saw him leaving and called him a b****. He was gone and ran out of the back door before we could get to him. My mom played no games when it came to me and she never let anyone bother me. I could have fought back and defended myself but because I was shy and never trusted a lot of people, I didn't. It wasn't until years later when I started to have trust in people.

My mom was my everything and I loved her for who she was. She was the provider like my dad was. I was a mama's boy. I leaned on my mom for moral support and she needed me. I needed to be strong for her more than ever. She was going through a time when she was depressed and it was hard for her. I was trying to help her, but she could not be helped. It was bad for her but there was nothing I could do. It hurt me because I wanted my mom to live a long time. When it comes to life, it is easy to become selfish. Her health began to decline over the course of three years from 2009-2011. The more she was depressed, the less she lived. She was a stay at home mom, raising me, my brother and sisters. My mom never drove a car, as far as I can remember. She could have had her license but she used public transportation or family.

My mom had a husband that loved her unconditionally and her kids. Like I said earlier, she was a hard-working mother who was a no-nonsense type of a woman. I like to think back on the good times when my mother, my twin sister and myself spent time with my aunt and her family on Fridays. We went over to my aunt's house to hang out and watch TV. Another issue mom had to deal with was her health. It was March 2011 when she became very sick and I remember a conversation we had where I told her I loved her. The next day, it was school time and I had to go. This was my last year of high school and I had to finish. I knew that I wanted both of my parents at my high school graduation. It was painful to know my mom, would not be there. Mom was given a choice, due to her medical condition, to stop smoking and drinking but she did not listen. She knew she would leave behind loved ones that cared about her if she did not quit. That night when her and I spoke was the last conversation we had. It was late one morning on March 15, 2011 when my mom was found unconscious. I could remember waking up and hearing screaming and crying. My dad was panicking about what happened to my mom. My dad loved my mom and was there for her until the very end. It was a horrible experience for me to see his love, my mom, stop breathing. However, I will never forget that moment in time. I had missed school the whole week. My mom was in the hospital for three days before she was gone. I was graduating high school months after she passed.

In January of 2012 my dad became sick. He had developed Leukemia and was having symptoms from the illness. He would get the chills and sweat in his sleep. Dad was not himself while he was sick. He hid his illness for ten years and no one knew he was sick. It was truly sad that he kept it from family and friends. My father worked through his pain and did not let his illness affect him. He had a lust for life and fought to live as long as he could. He never wanted anyone to know he was sick. I admired him for pulling through, even though he needed rest. Dad was the type of guy where he did not let anything get him down and he found a way to get things done in continuing to work despite his illness. He will always be my hero and he made me the man I am today. When he and the family got the news, I could not remember how I felt at the time, but I could imagine I was hurt. It really devastated me that he kept his illness from me. I had no idea for ten years he was very sick. It was hard to tell what he was feeling on the inside. Again, he was a fighter and he did everything he could to beat his illness, be there for his family and continue the business he ran.

Dad ran his own business for over 20 years. He sold fragrances and incense and he had his own slogan, "You unique with mind" or something like that. He ran his business from our house and sold his products from upstairs. He ordered and sold incense instead of making them himself. My sister Elle and I would bag up incense into packs of 25. I mostly did labels and the incense were named Williams Unique Incense. Dad would sell the incense for one dollar. He unopened the delivery box and unpacked the incense himself. He gave Elle and I incense to pack in clear bags. We would count out 25 sticks, label the incense and then the remainder were kept in clear packs.

Dad usually went door to door to sell the incense and I went along with him to learn the tools of the trade. His customers trusted him and his product, which helped keep his business going and made all of us happy. He felt he could work and run his business to the best of his ability and was teaching me the game of business so one day I would work for myself. Dad worked for himself and never worked for the "white man." He worked all his life but he really wanted to have his own company. He was the best businessman around Fort Wayne, Indiana. Sometimes, I may not have liked how he showed me things but I knew he was only trying to help. He was very strict on getting things done when they needed to be done. Dad was very old school in his ways which meant he was in charge and that was it.

My dad was hard on me because he wanted me to do well. Let's just say he played no games when dealing with common sense and business. Yeah, he knew a lot; he told me to never be afraid and always be a man and to always do what makes you happy. He cherished his days and never gave up during his sickness. Even when his family wanted him to not push himself so hard, he always tried to keep himself busy. I generally loved my dad. I still love my dad. One of my favorite memories with him was that we liked to watch the TV show *Girlfriends*. Dad used to love that show. He thought it was a funny show and saw me watching it. He would watch any show I watch. That was what I liked about my dad. He enjoyed watching TV with me.

On April 17, 2012 my dad, my cousin, and I drove to the hospital in Indianapolis for a checkup. At the time, I had no idea my dad was severely sick as he had not shown any symptoms of his condition. My dad was told that he was okay at the time and was given medication. All my dad wanted to do was get back to work and focus on his company. A month later, my dad was diagnosed with Leukemia. I found out that Leukemia is a cancer of the blood cells affecting the immune system. My dad's condition progressively became worse day by day. The disease eats away your blood cells making you increasingly ill overtime. It took several months for the medication to have an effect on my dad's illness which led to his remission.

Early one morning on October 9, 2012, the VA took my dad to

the hospital in Indianapolis. He had to go for further testing to find out his prognosis resulting in a month long hospital stay. One Saturday, my oldest sister, my niece and I went to visit him. We were all able to catch up and there were lots of laughing and joke telling. Dad helped raise my step sister and step brother. We grew up with the same mom. My step sister and step brother had a different father. After a few weeks or months of treatment, he came home still sick and did not look like himself. He had to wear a mask as he could not get myself and my sister sick. My sisters helped take care of my dad and it took a while for my dad to recover and go back to work.

Dad was happy to be working again, as it was all he wanted to do. He worked for what he had. He worked from sun up to sun down. He continued mowing lawns and sometimes let me help him with the bigger yards. This was a great way to be able to spend some quality time with him. The chemotherapy my father was going through took a toll on his body. He began to lose his hair and quite a bit of weight. My family knew he was going to die soon. However, he continued to work through his illness but unfortunately, we knew it was going to progressively get worse.

Cancer is a scary thing that just creeps up on you. I mean, cancer is unexpected like most illnesses or diseases. My dad was very lucky he tried to live right. He changed his life for the better. My dad is still my hero no matter what. He really tried to live his life to the fullest and never complained.

I would never wish anyone's parents to go through what I have gone through with my parents. I have gone through hell with losing my parents. My advice would be to always cherish your parents and never disrespect them. Love your parents for all you have because they are all you have in this world. They mean everything to you. I just want to say how dad lived his life before his death. I really want to say how much I loved him. He was very important in my life and how he changed my life for the better. I had my dad to help me get ready for life and it was a lot on him. He was my hero because he still had the strength to make things happen for me. He was always someone I really admired and he meant everything to me.

I have gone through a lot with my dad. I spent a lot of time with my dad when he was cutting yards and selling incenses. He was running his own business for over 20 years and was very successful. Dad was a well-respected man. He was loyal to his word and was faithful with everything he did. He instilled in me at a young age to always be real with people. It is the only way that anyone will respect me. I have always found that people will believe you if you do.

Me and my sisters took care of our dad and made sure he was OK. It was a traumatic time for that situation. I did not want to lose my dad. Not knowing when I would lose him broke my heart. I will always remember my birthday on May 2, 2013 because it was the last birthday I spent with my father. Dad, my twin sister and I had lunch at a local restaurant. I remember having chicken fingers and fries while we had good conversations. Later that week, dad drove himself to Parkview Hospital. We were uncertain about the outcome might be. I was not prepared to lose my dad so soon. He spent five days in the hospital and was surrounded by his family. My sisters and I went to the hospital to see him not knowing that it would be our last time seeing him alive. He was loved by his family and he passed away with his family by his side. I cried into my cousin's arms. He passed away on May 6, 2013.

My mom and my dad's funerals were emotional. The funerals went by smoothly and all my immediate family and other family members were there. I listened to everyone speaking and heard remarks from loved ones. They knew my parents and loved them. It made me feel loved that they knew my parents for who they were. I got the courage to get up there to read my poems about my parents. My dad originally helped me write the poem for my mom. I since made another poem that mentions my dad. I was crying during the poem and it was difficult to read my poem. I got through it but it was very hard.

December 14, 2015, I wrote letters dedicated to my parents which explained how much I missed them. I recalled a lot of difficult times and pain that I had to experience from their passings. It has taken me time to come to terms over each of their deaths. I still miss my mother and father to this day. I want to share my letters to my parents and how much I miss them.

Here are the letters I wrote about my mom and dad:

Dear Mom,

Words cannot express how much I really love and miss you. It has been four years since I saw you here and it is very hard. I know something wasn't right before you left and I wanted to tell you I love you. I really wanted you to be there for me when I graduated high school and went to college. I can't say how much that would mean to me to have had you there.

You left hurt and sorrow in my heart. The way you died was not fair at all and it hurt me the most. You could have changed the way you handled situations. It still leaves me in shock how you passed. I hoped you would come out of your coma and it would be alright, but you didn't. I still to this day don't like reliving how it all happened to you.

You left something in my heart that I cherish the most...Our good memories together as mom and son. I remember our time together. We enjoyed each other and you were a good mom. I terribly miss everything you did for me. I miss your cooking every week. I miss Sunday dinners the way you make them taste good.

It has been so long that I remember when you cooked a meal. It has gotten me all emotional that you can't do that anymore. I know you are happy and in no more pain. I believe you wanted me to keep going in life and never stop. For that, I love you, Mom.

Sincerely,

Your son Daniel

Dear Dad,

Words cannot express how much I terribly miss and love you. You are a very true man of God. every man should look up to you. I look up to you, my father as the man that you are. Dad, you meant everything to me and I truly loved you.

You meant the world to me and you were my best friend. I think about you all the time and where your life could have been if cancer had not killed you. I just could not have come to terms with that you were sick. It was very painful to see how you were. You were a lot stronger. It was just so hard even now talking about you. You were a fighter. You became stronger before cancer. You taught me to never give up on myself and I always would make it through life. You made it through your whole life. I love you dad for your courage and determination in life. You could make a situation turn out good and with the little that you had. You were one of a kind and can't be replaced.

I know you loved me and would have always been there for your family. You were unselfish about the way you were. You were a stand-up type of a man. I can think of a lot to say about you but I will say you were the best father I had. We spent a lot of time together that I will never forget. This man was you and I honor you every day and wish to speak with you once again. You were that most admired because you got yourself together for the family. You had a past, but you had changed for the better. You loved me, my sisters, and my brothers and especially loved your wife. I really want you to know I still love you.

Sincerely,

Your son, Daniel

Chapter 2

My Friendships and Relationships

On a lighter side, over the years since I have been on the internet, I have met a lot of guys for friendships. I talked to them for contact and communication...just getting to know them for who they are. I enjoy it because it's easy to get into contact with them. I have their phone numbers and I can call them when I want. I really like to talk to my friends online and I made a lot of them. I have been a part of social media since 2007.

Some of those guys were involved in relationships and sexual relations too. I noticed there were sites about men who just wanted to hookup. There was one site that I did like that was similar to MySpace which I used to have but not anymore.

I have YouTube but I haven't made a video since 2011 or 2012. I made videos about my life and it was called The Daniel Show. It has been sometime since I made a video about what I am up to. I need to get back to making videos. I talk mostly about myself, my writing, and where I am in life. I felt very dedicated to making movies about my life.

I recently found gay groups on Facebook that are for people in Indiana and older men. They are a fun way to meet new people and learn about their interests. I enjoy it because you get to chat with men 18 or older. Some of the guys on there want to find love and some want sex. I had shared nude pictures with guys and it was something that I knew better than. I was curious to expose myself and it got me in trouble. It was not a pleasant experience.

I have worked very hard for my freedom to come back to me. I had an incident a few times while I lived in the waiver home. First, I exposed myself on the internet on some gay site. I just wanted to share that about my choices on the internet. I had stalked a guy who I thought was cute and gay. I thought he smoked cigarettes because some Arabians or Iranians smoked. He saw me a few times peeking through his window. To make a long story short, he called the police on me and staff got involved. I learned my mistake and getting caught with my behavior. This is behind me for now and never to be resurfaced again.

I had a few guys that I like who I have gotten to know. One person I knew was a guy named Ted. We met on Tagged first and then became friends on Facebook. He was older than me and passionately cared for me and always meant it. We conversed with each other and really hit it off. We still care about each other. We had been talking a lot about how much we loved each other. We had been so busy that we hadn't talked on the phone. We missed each other and wanted to be together. I wish I could see him again. He visited me before at my apartment and it was good.

On February 13, 2015, I met a cute guy and we became friends. We met at Walmart for the first time. The guy was six foot and was Asian. We exchanged numbers and started talking.

I found him on Facebook. This particular day I was off from Arc. Since then, I haven't heard from him.

Rarely, I would meet people off social media sites. These days, you can meet anybody off social media sites. I like using Tagged because I can make new friends I have never met. It's cool that I can chat with different people. Over the years, I have made online friends. August 5, 2015 was the day I got to meet Ted for the first time. He was 6'1 tall with blue eyes and brown hair. We took pictures and got to know each other. We held hands and then we kissed in the hallway. I'll never forget that day when I kissed a white guy. I truly to this day care about him very much. I really miss him.

I met this guy named Darrin and he was a gentleman. He made me laugh and smile. He really has the nicest blue eyes I have ever seen. Darrin drives semi-trucks and travels a lot of states. That's one hard job. You are gone a lot of days sometimes even during the winter. I met Darrin during summer and we had a good time together hanging out. He was funny and had a great smile. I really did enjoy him a whole lot. He had asked me why I was so quiet when we hung out. He thought I was nervous with him. He read my body language well. To make the story short, we hung out twice and we met online. The first time we hung out was at the Taste of the Arts Festival. We hung out more and got to know each other. He asked me I could pay for his gas for driving me home. I felt bad that I couldn't help him pay for my ride there and back. I wanted our friendship to work. Today, we communicate through email and phone. Darrin and I talk here and there but he hasn't seen me in a while. I never meant to hurt him by not helping him that one night.

I had an online boyfriend named Brian and he was 18 and very cute. I wish he was older his age was appropriate. He was a white guy and tall. He was just right for me and I loved him. I cared about him as my friend and lover. I have this to say I did like him so very much. Even though we met, we should not have stopped talking. I never dated a tall guy before and he was so cute. I really do hope we talk again and he comes to see me. He sounded sincere and wanted to give me a chance.

In 2015 I started to become involved with the Lesbian, Gay, Bisexual, Transgender, Queer (LGBTQ) community. I have mentioned before about coming out in my past. I have been a part of Fort Wayne Pride for 2 years now. I haven't been on the committee but I have been involved going to events. I went to almost every event in the last two years. My staff took me to most of the events. Usually, they have Thursday Night LGBT socials at Pint & Slice. I go to that every third Thursday of each month. They usually talk about topics related to LGBT rights, such as the history of the Fort Wayne LGBT community. I never knew a whole lot about Fort Wayne history of LGBT until I went to the meetings. The last meeting, I went to was back in February 2015.We usually played games in the meetings from what I remember.

I like that you can be open to being who you are and never be ashamed about it. It hasn't always been easy for me being gay since I have come out. I came out when I was in high school and it was hard. My parents didn't know who I was and they only knew I liked older men. My dad knew I had liked older men. He didn't accept my decision to be with older men because he always told me to stay out of grown men's face. I didn't listen, which made our relationship rocky for a while. It was worth having my relationship more with my dad than being with men that never cared for me. Even now, this would have been a better choice to have made up with my dad. My dad did not deserve that at all.

As I have said, I just can't live with regret about what had happened. I can't allow my past to stop me from my future. I respected my father for what he was doing for me. He wanted me to be safe and not get hurt. All fathers want their son to be in love the right way and not get hurt. My dad wanted me to be in love with a girl but my heart was not in that. I believe my dad would have been hurt by what I have done with myself. I know he loved me for being his son, not just what he wanted me to become. It does seem like at times I do have regrets about the choices I made and I am learning to get over that. My dad could not change the way I was but could encourage me to live right. That was all he could have done.

I have been working on learning how to date guys my own age. I know some of them won't commit to a long-term relationship. All they look for is "having fun" as the young people of this new generation would say today. All the young people (ages 18-25) usually look for sex. I'm just being honest about it though. While some young people who have their hearts set out on being loved or being in a real relationship. A majority of relationships it seems are short term and don't last very long. Some relationships last with their soul mate who commits because they give their all. When I mentioned that all young gay men look for is sex, I meant that they look for unhealthy encounters with guys. I have experienced guys who look for a good time on the internet and in person. I can remember one time when I met a guy online and he was secretly straight. We conversed and got to know each other. He would have been legal...at least 18 years old. I'm not writing all his business so I am respecting that. He was trying to chill and come over and I told him no. I was not looking for that...just 'Chilin'. Long story short, we never talked anymore. He ignored me on Facebook after I wrote to him.

I have not went as far as having actual sex. I don't believe there is love in anal sex. I just can't take the pain in that. I have seen it before and I just don't have that ability to become desperate like that. It just is not for me. I have dealt with men who only wanted sex and I didn't know better. I had encounters mostly throughout my life and as I got older, I realized that that wasn't me. What happened to me when I was 15 or 16 was not my fault. I had to realize that I had closure from what happened. I don't see the guy who exploited me anymore and do not know where he is at today.

When I think about my future and about my future wedding, I just want a small gathering with only my sisters, brothers, and a few close friends there. I want my partner to have me as their friend and lover. We exchange vows and I want it to be special between us. I honor that and believe that will happen for me. I feel that in my heart that I was meant to be in love. My time will come for me. I just know it will happen when the time is right. Once it will happen, it will be exactly how I wanted it to be.

I had gotten the opportunity to meet new people at this Rainbow Bowling social This year, I have been becoming more involved with hanging out with the LGBT community. I went to a local event for Rainbow Bowl for Fort Wayne Pride. It was held at Crazy Pinz the night of February 23, 2016. I had a wonderful time bowling and I remember making a strike on my first try. It was awesome that I at least tried to play bowling. I got there and saw a lot of guys and girls hanging out at the bowling alley. I spied a cute guy who I really liked at the time. I noticed him outside smoking a cigarette while we were heading inside the bowling alley. We had a chance to talk and he was open to talk to me. I thought that was nice that he had taken the chance to talk to me. His name is Adam. He's a white guy, tall, easy on the eyes, blue eyes and slim built. We talked about what we had liked and about our families. We shared a kiss after we had talked. He was a good kisser when he made eye contact with me. I thought that was the best part of the night. We took a picture for Fort Wayne Pride. I asked all the right questions and was making sure I got to know him.

I haven't seen him since that night but we text and Facebook each other here and there. I reach out to him a lot and want to hear how he is doing. He always was happy to hear from me and glad to know what I have been up to. It was nice to have that type of friendship that we have made between us. I do enjoy how he has been open to talk to me and getting to know me. I didn't see him again for about four months. We finally saw each other at the Fort Wayne Gay Pride 2016. It was a Saturday night when I went to Pride and saw him. He had just gotten there and we talked for a bit. I wish I could remember what we talked about. He had smoked a cigarette while we were talking and took pictures. I still text and message him on Facebook. I still think about our friendship every day. I truly have always liked him and he knew it. We are friends to this day and we still stay in contact.

I looked forward to Fort Wayne Gay Pride 2016. I had volunteered during the two days of Pride. I had to leave several times to volunteer and go home. On Friday night, I got to go volunteer from 6:45-8:30 PM. All I had done was sell Fort Wayne Pride t-shirts and wrist bracelets. I got to watch people walk by as they were taking pictures and talking. I had my camera out to make videos and take pictures. I got to see people I haven't seen in a while like a former program manager from Bethesda. I got to talk to her for a bit and see what she had been up to. She looked different than before we worked together. She was very nice to me and she cared for me. I really have missed her a lot. We are friends today because of how hard she worked for me. That night, I didn't get to see DEV (a singer) perform which would have been fun. I had to go home that night. It was all going to work out the next day.

I got up the next morning, got ready to catch the bus and head downtown. I had gotten up and ate breakfast staff made me. I took a shower and got my clothes on. I went with my worker that day and roommate Troy and waited for the bus. I caught the bus in front of the apartment complex in Canterbury Green Apartments. The bus took me half way down town and I got off by the courthouse. I walked down by Headwaters Park to the gay pride parade. A lot of people were there to march during the parade. Protests were there and it seemed to be intimidating for most people who wanted love and peace. There was hate and anger toward the gay people that wanted to fight for what they believed. We had to fight hard and take a stand for love and equality in this world. We want to feel accepted in this world and let no one take away the right for us to love who we love.

The parade started around 11:15 or 11:30 AM and went all the way around the Martin Luther King JR Bridge. We walked long ways through streets and bridges. It felt good to be heard that we mattered in our community that love exists with gay people. I felt proud that I got to march in a parade for what I believed in. I always wanted to have the chance to be a part of something that

I knew would make a difference in my life. I felt proud afterwards when the march was over. I spent the entire day walking around, meeting new people and volunteering. I had to go home and rest before I went back to volunteer for a while. I got back there and volunteered doing the same thing (selling t-shirts and bracelets.) I got to hang out with people who helped sell the shirts and bracelets. It was very hot that weekend while I was volunteering. I had felt anxious to get out and see people at the pride fest. I really thought about not volunteering this year at Pride. I must confess that I would have enjoyed just hanging out with people and just having a good time. I had to wait to get off and have time and enjoy myself.

I had to go home and take my medicine before I could come back and get ready for the drag show on Saturday night. I went to the drag show with a staff member. I have seen a lot of drag shows but had never seen an actual big performance. I have seen a lot of performers who dance like the celebrity singers and you can hardly tell they are men. They are men and perform like they know all the dance moves. It was awesome that I got to see the drag show. I really did enjoy myself for the most part. I got in for free because I was a volunteer. Me and the staff member were there until 11:30 PM at Pride. Next year, I will be at Fort Wayne Gay Pride but I won't be volunteering. I will have a lot of fun and enjoy myself. Next year will be a lot better for me to meet new people.

On June 4, 2016 I went out to Babylon (After Dark). They

usually have drag shows on Friday and Saturday nights at the gay bar. It was my first time on a Saturday night going and I had fun. I got to meet new people from Babylon and take pictures with the drag queens. I usually go on Saturday nights to the drag show. It gives me a chance to relax the night before so I won't be so tired. It was my first genuine experience being out in public. It was out of my comfort zone and I never thought I could handle being at a bar with people. Some people don't talk to you or just walk up to you. You have to go to them and talk. That was hard for me when I had to approach people for a conversation, especially guys I never met before. It was an out of body experience to overcome speaking to people. I wondered how I would start a conversation with someone. I would be like "Hi, how are you doing?" and they would respond. Some guys would get into a lengthy conversation and some didn't speak a lot. It would be a hi and bye. You have that happen in conversations today.

I have worked on approaching people before I have something to say. I have done an excellent job not interrupting a conversation with a person. I don't like being rude and making a conversation be all about me. I want the person to have the ability to say what they should say. I'm very unselfish with other people and their feelings. I learned that a lot this year that I have reached out to people for conversations. That is something I should be prouder about. I have the courage to speak up and really talk to people without being scared. I still have years to go and hopefully my courage of speaking to people will get better. It takes time to get it right. Speaking to people, especially when you have a disability, is not easy. I used to be scared and not know what to say to people. I had to think about how I would say things that I was feeling at the time, or I would write down what I wanted to say. That sometimes would help me start a conversation by writing down ideas.

Overall, most of 2016 of me being a part of the LGBT community has been great. I have been more involved with being a part of something that helped motivate myself. And I knew that I could do it all on my own. The Gay Pride was sponsored by Fort Wayne Pride and they were a lot of people there. Cute guys I should say which was always a plus. I had met the cutest guy there. He was white and was tall like 6'1", I think. I loved his eyes and we got to talking. I could tell he was a bit shy and didn't know what to say. That was okay. I handled myself well when I asked questions and just got to know him. I will just say now that I do have anxiety and nervousness when it comes to meeting new people. I usually go up to people I never met before and just really be into the person I'm speaking to. This guy's name is Adam and we are just friends. We talk on Facebook and see from time to time how we are.

As far as my love life is going, I have talked to someone special that I really like. We never met before but he is cute and I really like him. We just have met through a friend of mine who works with me. We just now have been talking and getting to know each other. This has been recent as I have been writing this book. He is a white guy who is close to my age and lives in Fort Wayne, Indiana. He is an artist and a writer as well. We share writing in common because I also like to write. I am excited to see where this goes soon. We have talked about hanging out and going to the art museum.

Right now, I have been working on myself to realize what it is that I want in a man. I know that I have been working on myself for a long time and been patiently waiting. Now, I have decided to work on me because I have been hurt by meeting men who just want sex. I know there are guys my age and guys older who really are looking for love. I only have one life to live, and I know there is love out there somewhere for me. I really don't want to be single a long time. I should allow God to keep my mind straight for someone who will love me for me. I have my whole life to meet someone. I feel days go by and I need someone to make me happy. I deserve someone special that will support and appreciate everything there is about me. I should continue to stand for what I want in a person and not allow anyone to change my belief in dating someone special.

Chapter 3

My Living Situations

After I lost my dad, my oldest sister asked me if she wanted me to stay at her house for a while. I only stayed for 2 weeks and she wanted me to leave. She was gone for a week because her family member was graduating from school. My twin sister, her girlfriend and I were in her house while she was gone. She came back that next week but I did not stay that long. I went from home to home and I was trying not to get in a waiver home. I stayed at my brother's mother's house. She had a big house and a room for me. She had a salon in her house where she did hair for a long time. I stayed there for a few days and my brother came down from Columbus, Ohio for a week as usual. I really miss my brother and haven't seen him for some time. I was going to visit him sometime because I wanted to see my brother.

My cousin came over to Mrs. Davison's house to see if I wanted to live with him. I did not know what I was going to get into. I was going to say no but I had nowhere to go. I said yes and was going to live with him. He lived with his wife and his mother in law and thankfully I got along with everyone. It took time for me to get used to living there. It was all good in the beginning with my cousin. We got along for the most part but as time went on and we did not get along. It got to a point where it was really bad. I made the mistake of living with him. We got into arguments and put each other down. I did not know if he was okay with me being gay or not. I don't know if he was homophobic or against gay people. I can't speak on what he believes, only how I felt. He was upset that one time I called a guy from his house phone.

Cousin Joe allowed me to spend time with family. I got to see my brother in Ohio. My sisters came and took me to see him. I went to church with my cousin and her family sometimes. The church is called Kingdom Door Christian Worship Center. I was going there for almost two years. My cousin, my uncle (the Pastor) and my aunt (the First Lady) still go to that church. I have not been back in a long time. After my dad passed away, I tried to go to church and really see if I enjoyed it. I did feel at home at KDCWC, but it was not the way my dad preached. My dad had his own church (it was a small church.) My dad spoke from the heart and from the Word.

Cousin Joe wanted me to live with my other cousin Tina. I really wanted to live with Tina. She wanted me to live with her for awhile. I left my Joe's house in September 2013 and lived with Tina. I believe it was September 9 when I moved in with her. I had spent the night over at her house a few times. She had health problems with her kidneys. She was missing a kidney and I prayed she would find a donor. My uncle and aunt grew up with my mom and dad. To this day, I miss them for the family that I once had. They helped me get more involved in church.

Living with Tina did not last long. I lived with her from September 2013 to October 2013. We were at the hospital when my cousin told me I was going to live with my oldest sister again. I started living with my sister that night and my twin sister Elle was home at the time. We were watching The First 48 (my sisters Joy and Elle liked that show.) As far as I can remember that's what we did that night. Joy works as a nurse. She works day shift and mornings. Sometimes she works weekends to make extra money. I always thought she could be an in home nurse, but that was not for her. A few weeks later, Joy, her son and I went to Texas to visit my cousin, nephew, and niece. We left that Tuesday and came back that next Tuesday. We went to Desoto, Texas and stayed at my cousin's house. Desoto was really nice. That was my first time down in Texas. I really liked being in Texas and what it had to offer. There is a lot to see and do. Texas is much bigger than Indiana. Desoto is about fifteen minutes away from Dallas. Aside from my trip visiting Grayson in Ohio, this was one of my favorite vacations.

It had been six months since I last saw them. The last time I saw them was in May of 2013 at my dad's funeral. We stayed at my cousin's house. She has a very nice house that is far from her momma's. It was twenty minutes from Lancaster, Texas. Texas is on the Gulf Coast and one of the hotter states. There was a lot to do in the city. Joy, her son and I stayed in Texas for five days. It was a good get-away. While I was there, I attended football games and went shopping at Walmart. It felt just like home. There was a lot of shopping outlets and places to eat. My hope is one day to come back to Texas. I love warmer weather better than colder weather. I don't travel a whole lot but I really want to go back and explore Texas. Other cities I have visited are in Minnesota, back in the summer of 2003 my sisters, momma, my sister's family and I stayed up there. It was the first time I left Fort Wayne. It was our first family trip without Rob. My family and I stayed in Saint Paul and I wish we got to explore Minneapolis more.

Like Desoto and Dallas, there was a lot to do in Minnesota. A lot of places to eat, resorts, hotels, beaches, lakes, important buildings. I always wanted to go back to Minnesota to see how things have changed. My sister took us around to see the different places in Minnesota. What I knew in Texas were a lot of highways and detours to get downtown. There were a lot of freeways from one area to another. It would have been very hard to find if you did not know where you were going. My sister had to change lanes just so she wouldn't miss her exit. This was when she came and made it through Texas.

There were some Mexicans restaurants we visited, one in particular called On The Border that served Mexican food. I don't really care too much for Mexican food but I want to open up about my Autism and its effect on the way I eat. I was frustrated that we went to a Mexican restaurant. I felt there was nothing good for me to eat. The restaurant was able to make chicken tenders and fries for me. Overall, the trip was a lot of fun and I do want to come back to Texas, mainly because I enjoy the warmer weather.

Our family became closer once I got to stay with Joy. I felt connected with my sisters. I wanted to have a better relationship with Joy. I had to learn how to let go and have boundaries with her. I love her, even to this day and she knows that. She meant a lot to me and felt at that time I needed her. I know that my brother/sister relationship is real. It took a lot for us to be close again. It didn't last long before not only I felt disconnected to my oldest sister, but also to my sisters.

In March of 2014, Joy and I looked at houses through Bethesda Lutheran Communities and they had houses that were located north and south of Fort Wayne. I never saw myself living that far away. We looked at houses and had no idea where I was going to live. My sister and the area director at the time were filling out paperwork for me. I was going to live on my own that May. On May 8, 2014, I moved to a home in Garrett, Indiana. Prior to this move I used to live in a waiver home for Bethesda Lutheran Communities and used to go to Easter Seals Arc during the week.

I had been wanting to go back to Fort Wayne and live with my family but that didn't happen. I still to this day hated the way I lived in that home without my family. I don't know how I made it through all that time away from them. I felt that it was not my fault that I had to live in a waiver home and that I couldn't live on my own. I had been in a circumstance that I couldn't get out of. I am very glad that experience is over and I can live back in Fort Wayne. I had a roommate in July of 2014, shortly after he moved out and a new roommate moved in around December. My first roommate name was Stan and he wasn't a good fit for me. I really didn't get along with him and he took the attention away from the other staff members. He had behaviors which had an impact on me and I was late to appointments. I didn't like my roommate. We didn't seem to get along with each other. He treated me poorly. I really tried to laugh it off when he was in his moods. I had only known Stan for three months.

I had lived in Canterbury Green Apartments in Fort Wayne, Indiana for almost 2 years. I have to say that I never thought I would have lived in an apartment complex that I could afford. I shared an apartment with my new roommate, Troy. Bethesda Lutheran Communities provided the apartment for us. I liked it because Canterbury Green is near the area I grew up and is a nice community. I am more familiar with the southeast side of town and I had to get used to living up north.

For some reason, I have always enjoyed conversations with the Middle Eastern guys. I have met white guys as well. I have talked to black guys and a lot of them don't live out here at all. I know this does not sound like I'm a racist but I'm not. I love my race and embrace people who are my color. I happen to see a lot of Caucasian and Middle Eastern men that I have been talking to. I like meeting new people that are older than me. They have more knowledge. Sometimes, the Middle Eastern speak a language like "Broken Language" maybe not that. It's just hard for me to understand what they are saying. I have to say that I have done a lot so fun this year living in Canterbury Green. I like it here but will miss people and connections I made.

As time had went on, I hoped that he would had change his behavior. It is really embarrassing when he acts out. It was really especially hard when my family was not aware of what was going on. It had taken a lot out of me just to accept how he behaved. He never apologized to me when he acted up. I learned to laugh at his behavior because I didn't want it to bother me. Really, I needed to not let his behavior ruin my day. He only acted out when new staff were around. Moving in the house with him was not working. I had my eye on him. Troy, he became my new roommate. He was an older guy I lived with. I know his sister because she was my teacher aide for my Special Education teacher.

Since I lived in Bethesda, it has had its ups and downs. The good part is that I live independently some of the time. I get alone time to myself. I get my own room in the waiver home and don't have to share my room with anyone. The bad is that there are rules in the home and not having alone time with my visitors. The staff members... you must get used to them and deal with them. It has gotten me over two years of dealing with the staff members' personalities. I was really close to some of my staff members I had worked with. I really had cared for a couple of staff members that cared for me. I missed my former staff members. They have really been good staff that I truly cared about. I got along with my former staff members. I could go on and explain how much they mean to me. My former staff members are the ones that made sure I got to places, eat, and take my medication. I really had gotten close to staff and the female staff member I knew said she would never leave me.

I was not sure about if I was going to like it. I haven't been in a service where I was being supported or even noticed. This whole experience living in the company have been new to me. I just wanted to enjoy the experience in a service where you are being noticed having a disability. When I got into services with Bethesda Lutheran Communities, I knew nothing about their services. Well, I had a tour of homes where I could stay at. I can say how much of a change it would be a big change for me being with this company.

Over the last three years I have been with Bethesda, I have done fun things with the company. What I most remember was the parties Vance had during the holidays. I had been able to see different individuals and staff from Bethesda in Fort Wayne, Indiana. While I have been there, I can relate to some individuals of all disabilities, including those have the Autism spectrum. I have been high functional most of all my life. My parents didn't know that at all. My parents have been there to watch me grow until they passed away. Bethesda have been there to see me a few years. What can I say, this road of maturity don't come by fast. I had to work hard to pertain my freedom back and do what I had to do.

All the Bethesda employees help promote the parties and

see the individuals have happy faces. There are games, music, dancing and food there. I look forward to that fun time because you get to be around other people in your community. This company does a lot for most of their individuals to enjoy the events going on. That is what I look forward to when Bethesda can make a difference in an individual's life. So, I look forward to more holiday parties at Vance here in Fort Wayne. My favorite party of Bethesda I went to was the Christmas party. It was such a joyous time for everyone to come together with family and friends.

The Christmas party for Bethesda is usually at a church where staff, families and Bethesda employees be with the individuals. There is a sermon or bible reading from the pastor until there is a feast. Once the reading is done, then everyone goes in this special room where everyone eats and fellowship. Then individuals open presents from Bethesda employees and are happy. I always look forward to hear what I got and see what others got from Bethesda. It is truly special that Bethesda does care about their individuals.

Staff did take me out for dinner or go to the libraries. I usually go out when there is double staffed. I had 24-hour staff every day. Staff usually take me out during the time I got home from ARC or The Carriage House until I got ready for bed. This one staff worked with me from time to time. I had dinner of course in between. There were different staff members that took me out a part of my CHIO time. I got more involved in the community. I had missed that part from being a part of my community I served before. I had volunteered with the NAACP (National Association for the Advancement of Colored People) Youth Council. I served on the youth board to help bring awareness of youth getting involved in their community. I had a great time helping serve the mission to help youth in my community.

When I went to Easter Seals Arc, while living in Bethesda services, I went this one time to a Valentine's Day dance. All my friends were there and got to listen to music. I enjoyed myself and like that I got to see my friends from Arc. Staff took me, along my former roommate to the Arc dance. That night was fun and even though my worker had to be there, I had fun. This was the start I was going to gain more independence from staff. In 2015, I started gaining more independence from having staff around. I have now alone time with going out on outings by myself without staff. This is what I wanted all along since I have been in this program.

Over the last three years since I have been in this company, I have seen good and positive growth with me enjoying parties and outings at Bethesda. I really have become more outgoing and that I felt loved by being part of the Bethesda community. I can say that I have had fun during my time with Bethesda and have a lot of more fun.

I really had a bond with her and she was there for me. She was a close person I can talk to about anything and confide in.

She really spent time with me and cared for me. My other staff that I had was Jessica and she took me out to eat and the library. She really cared for me and she was an awesome person. She was the lead of my Bethesda home and she worked most of the week Sunday-Thursdays. She worked in my home a few weeks or a month when I came to the company. Aaron...what I remember most about them. One was black and the other was Asian. I saw Aaron (the Asian) the most because he was from another house with my former roommate two years ago. It was the same with Damon (black guy) who was only there two times working with me. Aaron was really nice to me and Troy and was young. I thought Aaron was much older than me when I first met him. He had looked older than me.

The first lead (worked with me) at Stonehedge (Bethesda Home in Canterbury Green) was Kisha. She was a staff member working with me and my former roommate in the beginning. She was super nice and cool. I still to this day miss her and she really did do a good job. Kim worked with me from time to time. She was cool and she really had a sense of humor. She cracks me up and makes jokes too. We are always on the go.

Mary was a very nice and polite woman. I got to spend a lot of time with her and we went to church and McDonalds. I got to hang out with her family and husband. She was a nice woman. She was Catholic and she went to church. Her faith was very important to her. She cooked most of me and Troy's meals during the week. She came to Bethesda in October, 2014 and worked with me and my previous roommate. Davon was working with me and Troy in mid-October- November 2014. He was at the office when I first saw him. He was quiet when I met him (he talked too). He was third shift staff and he's cool and chill. Me and Davon got along just fine and he is a guy that I respect. We hardly ever got to see each other during the week. He worked during the end of the week on Thursday nights until Sunday mornings.

I had a new roommate named Troy in December, 2014 who lived with me for three years. We got along a lot better than my previous roommate, Stan. I lived in Canterbury Green Apartments for 2 years. It was expensive to live out there and luckily, I shared the cost with a roommate. Troy is much older than I am and he came from another world. My family has been alright. I haven't seen a lot of them in a while except my sisters and brother. This was at Christmas time last December when I got to see them. My sister Joy had let me stay the night some of the time when she didn't have to work. I had wished I could spend more time with her than I do now. Sam was new and she had worked with me only since August, 2015. We have gotten along great and she really spends a lot of time with me. She worked with me and Terry in October, 2015. For the Bethesda Halloween party, in October, 2015, I dressed up as a socialite. It was someone who gossips so much. You usually dress up as a favorite costume, character, or someone you like. I thought that was cool I got to dress up like someone who knew a lot of information. It was just being that person that you want to be that day. I had fun dressing up. For Valentine's Day, there was a dance at Vance and the DJ was a program manager who worked with me. He played Mariah Carey because that is my favorite singer. He usually plays songs by her that I love. The song I like by Mariah Carey is Fantasy Remix. They have the place jamming with tunes everyone listens to

She feels like a friend to me. Terri started working with me in September 2015. She worked second shift and third shift. She is cool and kind like Davon. Adam started working with me on December 18, 2015. He is handicapped but he can do a whole lot for himself. He can walk, talk, drive and type on a computer. He got into a car accident but he is still alive. He has been recovering from his accident.

The person I have not talked about yet was a program manager for Bethesda Lutheran Communities. I still to this day really miss her and I am a friend. She was a fun and loving person. She has always enjoyed life and always been herself. I really like her personality and she really cared for me. That was another person that I got to spend a lot of time with. She picked me up to take me to Arc in the mornings. This is when I was living in Garrett. We went to get coffee at Starbucks in the morning. Let me clear one thing up...Arc was not the place for me. I had no desire to go there in the first place. It was not helping me become a man through that program. It really wasn't benefiting me in the least way. I had missed it a little bit because I made friends there.

Everyone had liked me for who I was. I remember I came out as being gay and it made me feel good. That moment is what I remember most about being at Arc. I had been going to Arc for one and a half years and I had seen a lot of changes.

In December 2016, my time at Canterbury Green Apartments ended. Unfortunately, I was not looking forward to living in another home with roommates plus Troy. I had two new roommates temporally. I lived out north in a home where again I felt uncomfortable at. It was so uncomfortable being in a home with a LOUD roommate. It just was not the right fit. We just did not get along and it was embarrassing. I kept wondering like at twenty-four years old I have a voice and I matter in all this. I should have never been in that home. The roommates I had was the one I lived with before, one that was an older guy and the LOUD roommate.

My staff changed again and had new staff. It was hard for me to experience the change in the home but I knew it was for a short time. I was going to live on my own with new staff. That was what I had to look forward to. It has been a long process for me to get here but I made it through. It took a while for me to get to this point. In February 2017, I started to live on my own. It has been a big change for me and I am grateful for it. During my time living in a service like Bethesda, I overcome a lot of grief. I have seen staff go, changes and different places. All in four years. I can say it was worth it to make it this far but it was not easy. Getting here took time and years but I made it. I cried some sad tears but now they are happy tears. I can truly be grateful for this chance to make it on my own. I would not be where I am at today without Bethesda.

This year also I really have done a lot of self-growth within myself. I really have overcome a lot of ups and downs within myself. It's like I been on my own the past year (2017.) I still have help with cooking, cleaning, and keeping up chores. But I have worked on goals with myself of being self-sufficient taking care of myself. I can say I have a long way to go before taking my life to the next step. There are things I still have to know about living on my own because it's going to be hard to make it out there. Bills, car note (if I have a car), food, supplies, everything. It would be completely different for me. It takes a while to get through the amount of work I put in than being in a waiver home.

Chapter 4

Easter Seals Arc & The Carriage House

I had went to Easter Seals Arc from April of 2014 until January of 2016 and have disliked it. Arc is a place for individuals who have disabilities. Easter Seals Arc is a place for individuals who have disabilities. January 25, 2016 was my last day at Arc. I had tried to enjoy my time being there and really did try to make the most of the experience. What I could remember at the time was how I had staff that come and go (like I did have that happened at home.) I had new staff that worked with me at Arc. All the former staff left. I really miss working with Karen at Arc. She always had known a lot of special projects for us to do. Former Arc staff were figuring out ways how I could succeed in the program. I had outgrown the program and wanted to venture out onto the next big thing. I didn't leave there on a bad note and really had made the best while I was at Arc. It was time that I go back and be more involved in my community again. I wanted to do more and have bigger opportunities. I did not like it because I was being limited so much. I had to ask if I could leave and go out of the building. There was a code that I had to input to unlock the door. (Since then, there is no code but should be.) We had staff watching us all the time and we were billed for our time. Our usual schedule for the day was free time from 8-9 then we had program hour from 9-11 until lunch. Lunch is from 11-12, then it is program hour from 12-2. Some days, depending on the weather, we would go out in the community for outings in the mornings or afternoon. That was how Arc worked.

It was time for me to work on myself and do more for myself. Jason, my mentor/friend/behavior consultant (BC) had recommended me a place that I would like and he was really helpful. This place is called The Carriage House and is for people who have mental illness or some type of depression. The Carriage House is involved in the community which I liked about the place. I had never heard of it before until my BC told me. I had an official tour of the clubhouse, which was January 26, 2016 and had started coming the next day. What I like about The Carriage House is that it is laid-back and you get to meet new people. I got to meet people from all walks of life and different personalities. I have gotten to socialize with people who can relate to me on the same path I'm going. We all need a little bit of help on the road to recovery.

From what I have heard about The Carriage House, it has been around in Fort Wayne, Indiana as a clubhouse since 1997. The Carriage House opened its door in May 1998. It has been recognized for having people to succeed with recovery in mental illness. The mission is that members feel better in their recovery to live in a better world. We all struggle with something and we all want to feel better. We have depression and anxiety and mentally can't handle circumstances that come our way. It is important for people with mental illnesses to take the road to recovery one day at a time.

I used to go to The Carriage House on Mondays-Thursdays usually at 9:30 AM until 3 PM. Now, I go to The Carriage House a couple times a week. When I was in a waiver home, usually the morning staff would take me. Lately, I catch the city bus. When I was living in a waiver home, a typical day would consist of getting up, taking my medicine, getting my clothes on, and eating breakfast and heading out the door. My roommate Troy got dropped off first before I did. Once I get dropped off, I would head inside and sign in and wait for the day of order tasks to happen.

The process of becoming a member consisted of getting a tour first to see if you like it. If you like The Carriage House, a staff member fills out paperwork and the applicant have to come three times within ninety days. Any three times doesn't have to be three straight days. Just three times. Once you are a member, you are a member of The Carriage House for life. The Carriage House is pretty laid back as far as being a member. What is cool is that The Carriage House celebrates holidays on the holiday like Labor Day, Thanksgiving, and Christmas. I think that is really cool.

The Carriage House helps with community supports (moving stuff in and out of homes and apartments), daily meetings to figure out the members and staffs day order tasks, house meetings, holiday parties, employment, so it is not like an institution that meets and talk about their personal conditions. The members help to support the other members and the staff, working side by side. I like that there are personal relationships with staff and members, you know how the members' day is going. Members interacting with other members and building friendships. It's great that I have been a part of being around members and staff members. It helps me become more social and really make new friends.

The Carriage House has unit staff on reception, orientation, and kitchen (ROK) and LOFT levels. Sometimes members and staff float between both units and decide where they want to be. Usually members decide which unit they want to work in. Whether downstairs, upstairs, or both, there is work to be done in clerical or in the kitchen. ROK consists of members working downstairs to set the dining room as a cafe for lunch, accounting, calling inactive members which staff and members have not seen in a while, and preparing lunch in the kitchen. LOFT members complete charts to document members' attendance, members' independent job records and Transitional Employment jobs. The Carriage House runs like a business, so the clubhouse is open Mondays-Fridays from 8 AM-5 PM.

I became an official member at The Carriage House on February 2, 2016. I have been a part of The Carriage House for a while now and been involved almost every day. It has helped me with my working skills and social skills. The support at The Carriage House have been great and I really like the staff members for being there and helping the members in any way. It was important for me to continue getting back to helping my community and share my story. If it was not for The Carriage House, I would not be the person I am today. I have met a lot of cool staff and members that can understand and support me in whatever I want to do in life. The Carriage House has forever changed my life.

In 2016, I have talked to members while I was at The Carriage House. I enjoyed their company and being able to get to know them. It's a community environment but I am careful meeting people. People are in their own world, some like to talk, be around others and some aren't. I sometimes can be by myself and not talk to anyone. I have done a good job being around other people. I just don't like being in a big room or crowd of people. I deal a lot with my anxiety and depression. Since I have been a member of The Carriage House, I have become active working and giving my time, so if I do decide to go back to work, I will be ready.

Chapter 5

My Thoughts on working again

The job experience working with a disability has been very difficult. I can say this first hand because I have overcome the ups and downs of working in a fast pace job environment. It is very competitive and very demanding.

I can say it has been very hard after 2 jobs in almost 2 or 3 1/2 years. The jobs didn't cater to human beings with disabilities. As a person with Autism and mental illness, I have been overlooked on what type of jobs. It is sad and complicated that I know I do not feel accepted with my mental illness. These 2 or 3 ½ years of working really changed my life. I was not fully prepared what work was on my own.

In my life, I considered working with my dad where he sold incenses and cut lawns. That was a business he had. It still has me wondering what work would be like without working with someone. My dad taught me the important lesson of working for myself. I took it as that I don't work for just anyone, but find my work to do. I always was amazed how much my dad worked half of his life before he gave up working for the "white man" he called it. He really wanted me to work for myself and feel proud of my hard work. My dad is still my inspiration to this day from me working hard.

I felt like all my life, I did not let Autism or any mental illness keep me from anything. I try so hard to not be hard on myself working. I like to feel a sense of pride and know that all I can do is my very best. That is what I always have lived by my very best. It helps me to ask questions when I need it and perform my duties at work. Autism kept me hidden for a long time until I finally accepted myself. It is very hard to battle a disorder that you cannot help.

The challenges of working with a disability are rough for me. There were days that I did not know how I was going to get through work. It got me through each day as a new start to complete my work. I can truly say that I have made it over jobs that kept me from giving up in the beginning. Now, looking back, I should have more time to really understand the real deal of work. It does take dedication and effort to work.

My first job experience happened back in October 2015 when I first applied at Taco Bell. I went in confident and knew I would get the job. I didn't realize it would be very fast paced and emulous with the work. There were employees there that I never met and started to get to know. There was an orientation, which included tests and I had to pass them. I had the help with a job coach. I had passed the quizzes and exams to be a "food champion." My job as a food champion was preparing food items, thermalize food ingredients (cold and hot). I thermalized the nacho cheese and beef. It was all packed and ready to be cooked at a certain degree. I cleaned, washed dishes and that was about it. I also took out the garbage for my shift. All of that made the time go fast at work. Mind you, this was my first job and I was being trained what I had to do.

I was working twenty-twenty-five hours a week at Taco Bell and had to make sure I was not going over the number of hours to work. It was part time; the job and it was working out for a few months. I started work officially, November 16, 2015. I had been working the Taco Bell close by my apartment, in Canterbury Green, for six or seven months. I felt the pressure to work on days where the work got to me. I felt that I was the only one working that dealt with my mental illness. Luckily, I had a team of employees that helped me get along with work. Some of the employees were not able to always help me. We had to work at a pace where food had to be sold fast. We had to get the orders made right and there were no mess ups. We were all humans and got orders wrong sometimes. I know I was capable of messing up.

The days I worked were the beginning early afternoons to late evenings. I could not work mornings or late nights because of my benefits. That was my downfall as the reason for me working now. I cannot work over certain number of hours or my benefits will be deducted. It is very important that I continue to work at 15-20 hours a week. It would be terrible for me to lose my benefits. So, I continued to work at Taco Bell and after a while, I just did not get supported entirely. I found that job on my own and soon, I received help from a company with Benchmark and a job coach. I was deeply disappointed and let down. I had enough and finally quit. I felt that I was not praised for my hard work. I had every right to walk away from the job and quit. It took me a while to let the job go but I can say that it was well worth it. It took me about six months to regroup and work again. I caution myself to be warned what I was getting into working. It became a lot for me to learn so much work at Taco Bell. I gain a lot of job experience because I never had a job before. My last day of working at Taco Bell was June 4, 2016.

I started working again in January of 2017. My most recent job was working for Aramark. I was working twenty hours a week; six hours a day on two or four days a week. This job was at the Memorial Coliseum. I was a utility worker and specialized in dishwashing. I hand wash the dishes and put them away. Usually, I would be in more than one space making sure the kitchen was neat. This job was the most stressful because it was a company a million-dollar company at that. The pay was good and raises every week. The first couple of days I got lost in the Coliseum. It is a big place with many entrances. I just tried it to see if I wanted to work. I had many regrets. There was also a position which I applied but was not available at that time. It became too stressful for me and all those times when I knew I could work, I doubted myself. I was to work until February 26, 2016 but I was let go February 8.

I had gotten off work late at night and I couldn't leave work until my job was done. I ran into trouble with my boss and chefs that were above me. I was working a slower pace than everyone else. That job was really fast paced and I tried to keep up the best I could. I stuck it out for a few weeks until it all became a lot of stress. I let the job go and put in my two weeks' notice but it was over for me after that. God helped me get through it but I stepped out of my comfort zone. I felt that my boss wasn't understanding my level of ability to work. They said I was too slow working and I was trying to work at a pace I could go. I don't regret ever working for Aramark.

The nice thing about The Carriage House is that staff help members get back to work again. It may be awhile but you get to go back to work. The Carriage House has Transitional Employment jobs, which are 6-9 months for a member to work at a particular job. It could be the library, a church, anywhere the member is comfortable working at. The assigned staff trains the member on the job for a few weeks until the member works by their self when they feel comfortable. Members gain independence and help from staff when they have problems working. Staff fill in when a Carriage House member is sick or not up to working that day.

After 8 months of not working, I decided that I would take on another job. I was nervous and almost didn't take it because my previous working experience with Aramark. At the same time, I felt trying to work was important and I wanted to give this job a shot. I got a job through The Carriage House Transitional Employment. The job I had worked was at Marshall's. It was a seasonal positional job. A staff member from The Carriage House was training me for the job and worked with me for several days I worked. The job position was me doing janitorial work cleaning the store. I had to clean the breakroom, clean the mirrors, pick up trash, dust the men & women shoe departments and dust the displays for seasons. I started out working on Mondays, Wednesdays, and Fridays from 12pm-4pm. It was a lot of people shopping during the hours and I had to clean. I had to catch the bus each day and staff would pick me up after I got off.

My first day working by myself after the staff member helped me out, was stressful. It was taking time for me to catch up on what I had to do. I had to do areas of the store on certain days. I always had to wipe down the mirrors before I started my daily tasks. I was working through the holidays like Thanksgiving and Christmas. My hours had changed since I wanted to avoid the customers at work. The hours were from 8am-12pm on the same three days. I had a consistent schedule, which worked out for me. I had to catch the bus earlier around 6:45 am to make it to the bus stop by the library. I get on the bus by 7:20 am and get off the bus to my job around 7:35 am. Marshall's opened when I got there and I waited in the break room to clock in at 8 am. I get a break from working at 10 am until 10:15 am, so, it was like 15 minutes for my break. I either have staff or my twin sister pick me up from work at 12pm. It was starting to get colder out and sometimes had to wait for the city bus to go home. I had to be on the bus until I got off close to home and walk to my apartment.

Over my 3 months working at Marshall's was different than the other jobs I had worked. It had gone by fast and I made friends while I was there, I had gotten along with my coworkers and the managers there. I could have seen my self-working for a while there. Unfortunately, the time I worked there had ended by December. Out of all the jobs I worked, I really did like working at Marshall's. Maybe not cleaning the store, but at least something different in retail. My last day working at Marshall's was December 29, 2017, right before New Year's 2018. I was going to miss my coworkers, the ones that I connected with in a short amount of time. I didn't miss any days of work except being sick one day. I am still proud of myself that I completed a job through The Carriage House. I didn't give up on myself even when I wanted to. That is something to be proud about.

The next job I get I will be more open to finding a job that will work with my hours, my talents, my goals, and creativity. God helped me through it all and I can say that I will not be rushed finding a job. I will take my time and really evaluate the job with the right energy, commitment, and being engaged (or that means the same thing.) Anyone reading this, if you have a disability or mental illness, don't let work or anything stop you. It just means WE must fight a little bit harder to be a part of the growing work population. WE, with mental illness matter in the work society. WE have a voice that can change how our boss and employers' minds see how we work. WE can't work less than other workers or we will feel less comfortable on the job. I say this because WE all with mental illness are not alone!!!

Me reading at the 2013 African American Read-IN at the Pontiac Branch Library in Fort Wayne, Indiana.

Me graduating from North Side in June 2011

Me at my open house party at my oldest sister's house

My money tree at my open house at my sister's

Me at the 2016 Author's Fair at the Allen County Public Library (Main Library)

My nice beard...thought I was handsome!

My photoshoot for my first book.

 Mr. G.Q. with that smile of mine!

 Me working out at Spiece.

My book promo for my first book

My book promo for first book

Chapter 6

My dreams of becoming a writer

I developed a passion for writing after my fifth-grade class, in which we wrote a picture book. I always knew I wanted to be a writer. I wrote stories every day about what I went through. Writing really helped me get out my thoughts good or bad. I started writing at the age of twelve. I wrote poetry and short stories about my life experiences. I knew it was my gift and it made me feel strong. People read my writing and are amazed by what I write. I wrote what I was feeling but wouldn't say to other people. I write nonfiction and fiction works. It gave me a voice to speak my mind. At the time, it was all about what I saw and I wrote it down. I felt proud of my writing and it was something I was passionate about. I wrote a picture book that was never published. I illustrated one picture book I wrote. I won a few awards for my writing.

This is how I got involved with my writing and how I have come to where I am today. I was so mad one night that I couldn't go to a school carnival, so I sat in the back of the house and started writing. It was an essay I wrote for Citizenship and placed Honorable Mention. That was a big accomplishment. I kept getting better and better with my writing. I had gotten help with my writing from a high school senior. It was a guy who gave me the idea for Brothers Stand Strong. The title The Choice of Living. I wrote about everyday life. That was my first book. I still want to promote it but it didn't get a lot of sales.

I read a lot of how-to writing books and it helped me out as well. This one particular book I read the one my dad bought home was *On Writing Well.* I really did enjoy the book and wish I still had it so I could refer back to my highlighting spots. I read a few other books over the years that help me with my writing. I still make mistakes of grammar and complete sentences but I'm learning as I go. That is what makes me a better writer. I write what I know and how I remember things that are around me. I write from what I see and what I truly mean. I write from a place where I am being myself and write out my words. If nothing else, writing is my outlet to get out my pain and saying my truth.

Since then, I won third place in a local poetry contest, was published in anthologies with other aspiring writers and was published in a book called Dancing with The Pen.

Chapter 7

My experience living with Autism

I still have my days good and bad with Autism. It is something I have made stride with and really have a long battle to go. 25 years of living with Autism has had its ups and downs. I dealt with my entire life in existence and capable of living a normal life. It is going to be different. I know there is so much for me to learn about Autism.

The biggest challenge having Autism is being able to develop conversations and new words. Using the same words over and over and pronunciation of words. I have struggled to change the conversation but come up words to say next. Especially when I'm talking to someone else. I am very educated and should never doubt myself speaking. I have to think first before I speak. It would be like I am asking something I want but can't properly ask it the right away. I have to process what I am saying first. It took years to think before I speak. It is just this part of what I am going through in my life.

Knowing the complications that come with Autism, I hope that one day I will be able to overcome those obstacles. What am I saying? I never know what the future holds for me. What I do want is to live the best life I possibly can. Boys suffer more with the condition than girls. Some of the people speak or don't never learn how to talk. I am one of the fortunate ones that can speak and process what people say. Most people don't have mental health issues and may not understand what it is like to live with a mental condition. I have had encounters with people and it is very hard to have them understand where I am coming from. The ones who understand are very encouraging to support people with Autism, kudos to them!

My eye contact has improved over the years. I couldn't keep direct eye contact with a person for a long time. I would stare at the person if I was noticing them. My problem was staring too much at people and I would get in trouble by my sisters when someone was speaking. I have since wore glasses because unfortunately, I can't see without them. Again, some people don't know who I am and never know that I have Autism. People do overlook me all the time not knowing what I am like on the inside. It hurts to go through that every day. I am so lucky that I am strong and not weak. I don't let anyone change the way I am or put myself at fault.

Another circumstance that I face being Autistic is rocking back and forth and fears. I rock back and forth when I am nervous and when I am excited about something. When something happens like a dental surgeon drilling my teeth (my teeth are sensitive) or a fire alarm going off. I rock back and forth when I listen to music and repeat the song on my phone. I can dance it's just I like to calm my nerves by rocking. My mom, dad and sisters had told me to stop rocking. They knew I could stop but it was struggle to keep my rocking under control. Imagine being in your own world and it's just you feeling the music. I dance like I never danced before. It has been a part of my condition and I still have to go through this. I don't want to be judged for rocking back and forth. I never rocked back and forth in public and try to keep it together. I get nervous especially when there are changes coming in life, when I meet new people, and my eating problems. I don't like a lot of noise and big crowds. I can't handle being around a bunch of people who push and shove. Loud noises like ambulances and bulldozers bother me.

I am a picky eater and I don't like a lot of food. I don't eat everyone's food because of certain textures or the way it is made. For example, spicy foods like chili and Mexican food like tacos and enchiladas. I don't like chili made in the winter time because I don't like the beans or the chili sauce. I don't eat that much Mexican food like tacos, burritos, enchiladas, etc., seafood, or mushy foods like potato salad. I have learned over the years to try new foods I have never had. The first time I tried fish it made me feel sick and I don't eat it anymore. One time, I threw up the fish my oldest sister made because I was eating too fast. Sometimes, I don't realize that I eat so fast, which doesn't give my food time to settle.

I talk to myself a lot and I notice that I think out loud. It could be voices I hear in my head. When I go to sleep, I dream about what I have experienced that day. The voices I hear are the voices when someone calling out my name. I wonder how I am able to process the voice people say when they are not around. The inner demons I have sometimes in me are not my fault. It is letting me know that I listen to voices just as some normal people. I don't know who the voices belong to the voices go in out of my head. The voices are always positive.

Sometimes, I can't sit down for a long time. I have to multitask and do something. Whether is typing on my laptop and listening to music at the same time, to cooking and looking at my phone. I know that is bad for me looking at my phone while I'm cooking. I really focus on reading a book sometimes, but my attention span keeps me from reading often. I used to read all day. It would take me a few weeks or a month to finish a book. I really try to comprehend and process what I am reading. I also listen to music when I am reading too. It calms me from what's going on in my life.

I don't do well with change sometimes. I know some things happen for a reason, but I don't know why. It makes me feel strong when I think about what I went through in my life. It is like one thing happens and then another thing and I can't recover. It would be doctor appointments or dentist appointments when I know are difficult for me. But the good side of things with my condition with Autism is I look towards positive outcome on life. That is what keeps me from giving up.

One other thing about my Autism is I don't like unwanted touching from person to person or food made to touch together. I don't like to be touched unless I am receiving a hug from someone. Gestures like unwanted touch makes me feel uncomfortable. It is hard to explain but most people with severe Autism, don't like to be touched at all. Again, I am one of the fortunate ones that I have no major issues with showing affection if I want it. I am a hugger and I do like to be hugged. I don't walk up to people to hug them without their permission. The person would not like that either.

Food touching bothers me when I eat. I have to separate my food and not have like certain food touching. I said in this chapter that I am picky with food and don't like a whole lot of food. I just don't like a bunch of food touching my meat and sides. I have a problem with that. I am just that kind of person that don't like a lot of food on my plate. Everyone is different with how they cook or have food on their plates. I don't feel bad about this at all.

Earlier in the book, I mentioned about meeting new people and how I have to overcome my shyness with speaking to people. Autism does play a factor with approaching new people. It is hard, I will not lie that it is scary to meet new people. Now, I really start approaching people and try my best to develop a normal conversation with that person. People cannot even tell that is cognitively wrong with me. We live in that society of people not knowing what Autism is.

After saying all of this, all my wants and needs matter to being a special needs man. I don't regret to this day of being someone else. I truly hope that one day people will not be judgmental and look past people with Autism or any medical condition. Whether it be physical or mental disability, we all deserve love and appreciation. We all live on this earth to be appreciated and kind to one another. My hope is that one day the world will have more awareness about Autism and the individuals with it.

Chapter 8

My growth as Daniel

I want to express that this book is about my struggles, my triumphs and my beliefs of what I have gone through. 25 years of living the best life I can possibly have. It has been my hope that I will continue to live my life to the fullest. I really want to thank myself for helping me becoming a better me. I know I am truly in a good place of finding myself and know where I am in my life. This is truly from my heart of who I am as Daniel. I will say that I have made a lot of changes in myself since I was young. I won't make this too long but I have said a lot in this book. I have overcome a lot of things and made my share of mistakes. I will let go here. I made it this far and I am not going back. I will forever be grateful for the changes I have made in my life.

It has been almost 4 years I have been working with a BC. His name is Jason and I have been working through my problems. He has been there with me mostly through the beginning and never left my side. He has been constant in helping me work through my issues with my family. He can relate to some things I have experienced in my life, especially with my sexual orientation. He kept it private until we formed a trusting relationship but I don't want to tell all his business in here. I just want to keep his life out of this book. I will say that he has been supporting me being openly gay and he respects that. I have a mentor and a role model in him.

I have been dealing with staff leaving and with my relationship with my family. I have been dealing with loss in my life and how I could overcome those problems. I have to breathe again and know that I will be alright. I have to take care of myself and know what I have to do. I have to make sure I can be alright first before anyone else. If I had not gotten help to recovery dealing with losing staff, my parents, and sometimes the relationship with my family, I don't know where I would be. Just making it through each day, physically and mentally, has made me a lot stronger. If I had not survived through living without my parents, I don't know where I would be. It has taken me awhile to get to this place in life. I really have worked hard to get to where I am now.

Chapter 9

My voice for the Future

I hope my life in the future is to become fully independent. My plans are really not having any more staff working with me and build more friendships. I want to make more friends and grow as a person with people. Before I was really shy and didn't trust a lot of people. Now, I seem to connect with others who like me for me. But still, I have to be aware that everyone is not meant to be a part of me or my life. No matter what. I cannot please everyone for what or who I am in life. That includes family and people I come into contact with.

Over 25 years of my life, I have self-reflected on what a life I have lived and still have more life to live. It could only go up from here and continue to become better. With that being said, what else I want to accomplish in my life I would be to continue working somehow. I want to get a job that will not be hard for me to complete. A job I could keep for 8 months to 1 year and really love it. A job I really love doing and keep the job for a long time. I do have to work on keeping a job and not quit it right away. If I'm going to not keep a job right away, then have another one in line is what people do. I had jobs where I just quit them without having another one. I have been told that by people having a second job while trying to quit your current job is important. The jobs I had were tough and was not easy at all. I worked at Taco Bell first, then I worked at Aramark and most recently, Marshalls.

I have to replace staff who works with me but have my own friends who will look out for me. I have to do better at not always having staff always involved in my life. I have seen a lot of staff that I have worked with come and go out of my life. I felt they should have not left. But then I have to realize they have lives to live. Friends who are in my life, that I talk to or see, are the ones who make sure I am ok. They message me on Facebook, call, plan visits, text me. That's the kind of friends I need in my life. One day, I want to build trust in the friends I have, but not just in staff members from Bethesda. Staff members are a part of my life for the hours they work and go home. It's hard for me struggling when I can't form a bond or friendship with them when they leave Bethesda for good. So, that is something that have bothered me for the longest time.

As much as I have fears to overcome that I want to achieve them and do it, driving is a long-term goal for me. It's scary when you have to know how to drive, especially it being your first time driving. I hope that one day I can remember where I am going on the road in driving and do my best. I got to keep my focus in driving and watch out for other drivers behind me. There are so reckless drivers in the world and car accidents happen. That frightens me if I ever get into a car accident and be paralyzed possibly. I got to think positive in knowing that one day I can drive. It is going to be a lot of practice me knowing my directions and signs for the driver's test. It will take me some time to catch on directions and signs I have to name on the driver's test. I can do it, just need to believe that.

All I want is to be in love with someone who wants me for me and be my everything. Someone that I can confide in and believe will have my heart. My boyfriend will support all of my dreams and I will do the same for him. Truly, it will be an honor to have my man in my life. When I get one who is faithful and understanding. Trust and believe, that is what I want in life. Another part of my life that I deserve to complete me. Got to continue to be myself and know what I want in a man. I have been working on myself for years just to make sure I am ready mentally, physically, and spiritually for a relationship with a man. Deep down, there is a good man out there for me. I pray and hope that true love will happen for me.

All of these things I listed I want to see myself doing in the next 5 or 10 years. However long I am on this earth, I plan to do everything I have to do to make my goals happen. I have experienced a lot of ups and downs but that has not broken me. I am still standing and will never give up. MY VOICE matters!

Acknowledgments

I want to first thank God for believing in me with my writing career. I am forever grateful for what he has done for me. Next, I want to thank my parents for their love and support. I wouldn't leave you guys out just because you are gone. You don't know how much I miss you guys every day.

I want to thank my immediate family my sisters Alisa, Sierra, and Danielle and brothers Jason and Glenn. I thank you guys for always supporting me and my writing.

Lastly, I want to thank my Facebook friends, my friends and family. I thank you all for supporting me in my writing career. I wouldn't be where I am today without you guys and I am thankful for your support.

Made in United States
Cleveland, OH
02 May 2025

16594871R00048